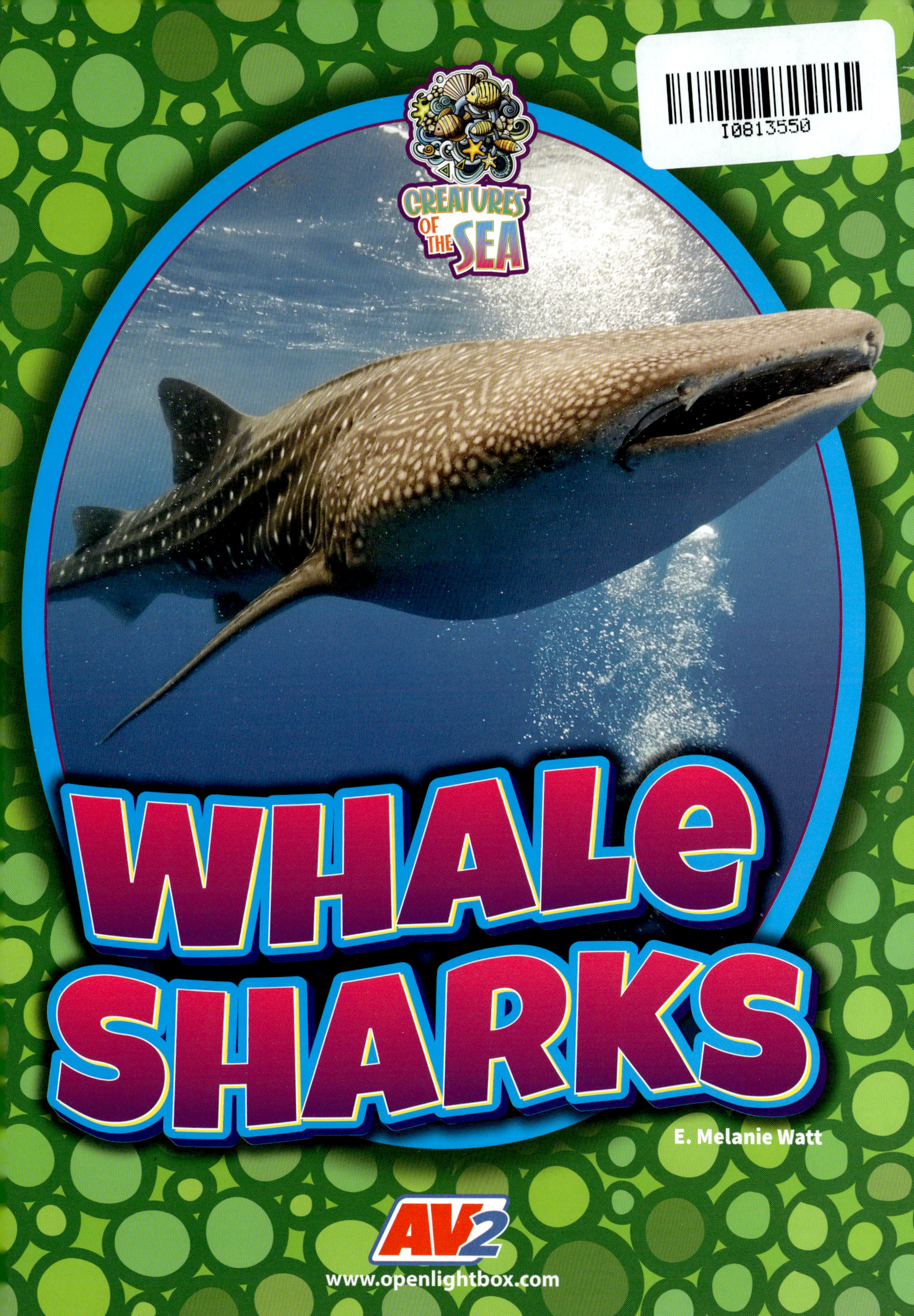
CREATURES OF THE SEA
WHALE SHARKS
E. Melanie Watt
AV2
www.openlightbox.com

Step 1
Go to **www.openlightbox.com**

Step 2
Enter this unique code
UCMRV6CKJ

Step 3
Explore your interactive eBook!

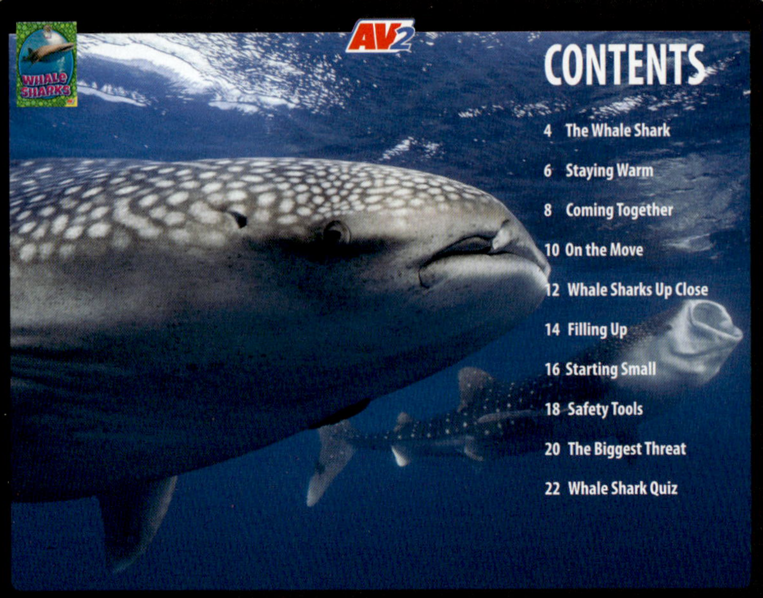

AV2 is optimized for use on any device

Your interactive eBook comes with...

Contents
Browse a live contents page to easily navigate through resources

Audio
Listen to sections of the book read aloud

Videos
Watch informative video clips

Weblinks
Gain additional information for research

Slideshows
View images and captions

Try This!
Complete activities and hands-on experiments

Key Words
Study vocabulary, and complete a matching word activity

Quizzes
Test your knowledge

Share
Share titles within your Learning Management System (LMS) or Library Circulation System

Citation
Create bibliographical references following the Chicago Manual of Style

This title is part of our AV2 digital subscription

1-Year K–5 Subscription
ISBN 978-1-7911-3320-7

Access hundreds of AV2 titles with our digital subscription.
Sign up for a FREE trial at www.openlightbox.com/trial

WHALE SHARKS

CONTENTS

AV2 Book Code 2
The Whale Shark 4
Staying Warm 6
Coming Together 8
On the Move 10
Whale Sharks Up Close..............12
Filling Up 14
Starting Small 16
Safety Tools 18
The Biggest Threat 20
Whale Shark Quiz........................ 22
Key Words/Index 23

The Whale Shark

Whale sharks are named for their size. Although they are the size of a whale, they are actually sharks. This means that whale sharks are fish. Whale sharks are the world's largest type of fish.

An adult whale shark can weigh more than 20 tons (8 metric tons) and be longer than a school bus. However, the whale shark is not dangerous to humans. It is known as the "gentle giant" of the sea.

Whale sharks have **swum in Earth's oceans** for at least **60 million years**.

Staying Warm

Whale sharks prefer the warm waters of the world's **tropical** and **subtropical** oceans. About three-quarters of all whale sharks live in the Indian and Pacific Oceans. The rest reside in the Atlantic Ocean. These big fish can be found both in the open sea and close to shore.

Much of a whale shark's day is spent within 500 feet (150 meters) of the water's surface. However, whale sharks have been known to dive more than 1 mile (1.6 kilometers) into the ocean depths. They tend to swim slowly through the water, at speeds of about 3 to 5 miles (5 to 8 km) per hour.

Swimming Speeds

WHALE SHARK
5 miles
(8 km) per hour

HUMAN
6 miles
(10 km) per hour

BOTTLENOSE DOLPHIN
22 miles
(35 km) per hour

Coming Together

Whale sharks are considered **solitary** creatures. Most of the time, they are seen swimming the oceans on their own. However, they will come together in places where there is plenty of food. These groups can have several hundred individuals.

Whale sharks often gather in large numbers when they **migrate** to their major feeding sites. For instance, the waters northeast of Mexico's Yucatán Peninsula attract close to 800 whale sharks in the summer. It is not known where these individual sharks are at other times of the year.

On the Move

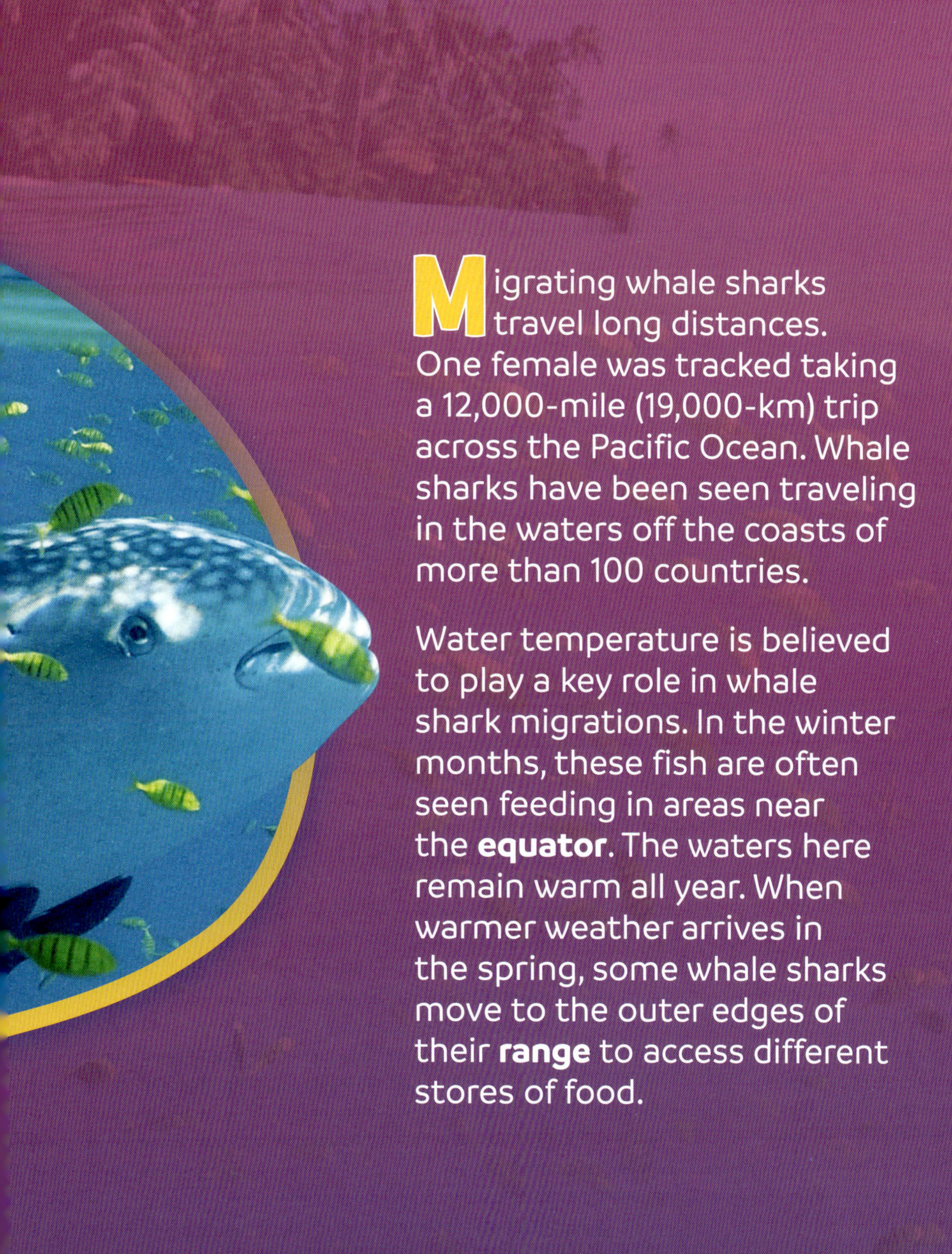

Migrating whale sharks travel long distances. One female was tracked taking a 12,000-mile (19,000-km) trip across the Pacific Ocean. Whale sharks have been seen traveling in the waters off the coasts of more than 100 countries.

Water temperature is believed to play a key role in whale shark migrations. In the winter months, these fish are often seen feeding in areas near the **equator**. The waters here remain warm all year. When warmer weather arrives in the spring, some whale sharks move to the outer edges of their **range** to access different stores of food.

Whale Sharks Up Close

Eyes To protect its eyes from approaching objects, a whale shark can draw its eyeballs backward into their sockets.

Mouth Having a mouth that is about 5 feet (1.5 m) wide helps a whale shark scoop up large amounts of food.

Gills A whale shark has five pairs of gills. These help it breathe by extracting oxygen from the water.

Skeleton A whale shark's skeleton is made of **cartilage**. As cartilage is more **flexible** than bone, it allows the fish to move easily though the water.
Dorsal Fins These two fins help keep a whale shark stable and upright in the water.
Pectoral Fins These fins help a whale shark steer itself through the water.

Filling Up

Whale sharks are carnivores. This means they mostly eat meat. Although whale sharks are big fish, they eat very small food. Their diet consists mainly of fish, eggs, and **plankton**.

Whale sharks do not bite or chew their food. Instead, they open their mouths wide, letting the ocean water flow into their mouths and out of their gills. **Filters** in the gills let only the water back out. Any fish, eggs, or plankton that were swallowed remain inside the whale shark's mouth. The whale shark then swallows all the trapped food.

A whale shark can suck in more than **1,600 gallons** (6,000 liters) of **ocean water per hour**.

Starting Small

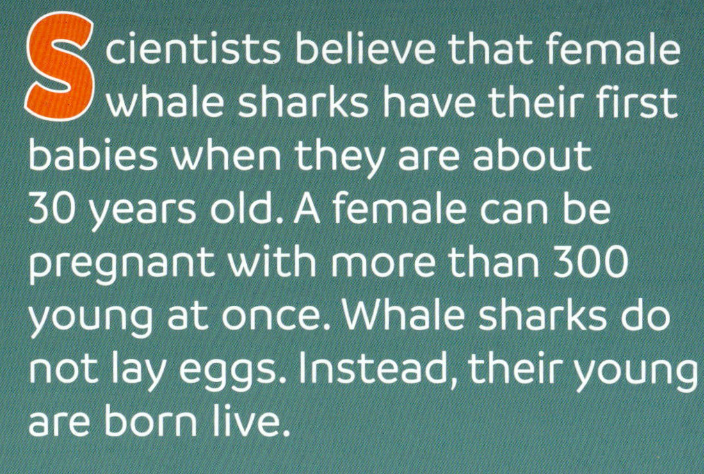

Scientists believe that female whale sharks have their first babies when they are about 30 years old. A female can be pregnant with more than 300 young at once. Whale sharks do not lay eggs. Instead, their young are born live.

Whale shark babies are called pups. The pups are not all born at once, as they are in different stages of development. Newborn whale sharks are about 1.8 feet (0.5 m) long.

Safety Tools

A whale shark has several features that keep it safe from **predators** in the water. Its size discourages most animals from attacking. Any that do attack have to bite through more than 4 inches (10 centimeters) of thick skin. A whale shark's skin is dark on the upper side of its body and lighter on the underside. This helps **camouflage** the fish in its watery home.

However, danger still lurks for younger, smaller whale sharks. They can be attacked and killed by great white sharks, tiger sharks, and orcas. Less than 10 percent of whale shark pups survive to be adults because of this.

Whale sharks that make it to **adulthood often live** to be about **70 years old**. Some can live up to **150 years**.

The Biggest Threat

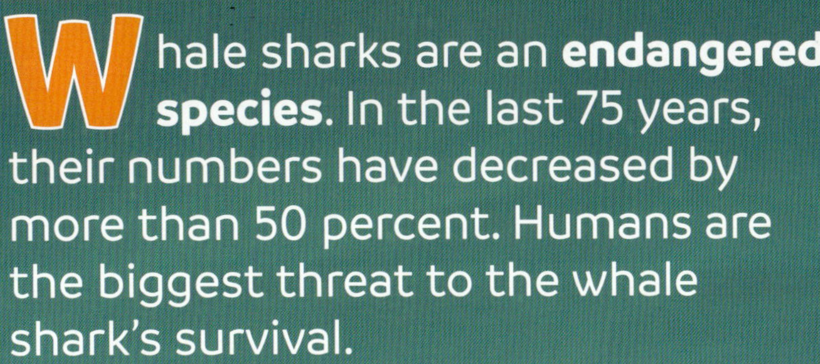

Whale sharks are an **endangered species**. In the last 75 years, their numbers have decreased by more than 50 percent. Humans are the biggest threat to the whale shark's survival.

These giant creatures have been known to accidentally get caught in nets set for other fish. They are also sometimes hit by boats traveling through their feeding areas. Plastics floating in the water can be dangerous if a whale shark swallows them when feeding. Many countries now have laws to protect whale sharks. These are helping to reduce the number of sharks being fished.

Population Decline*

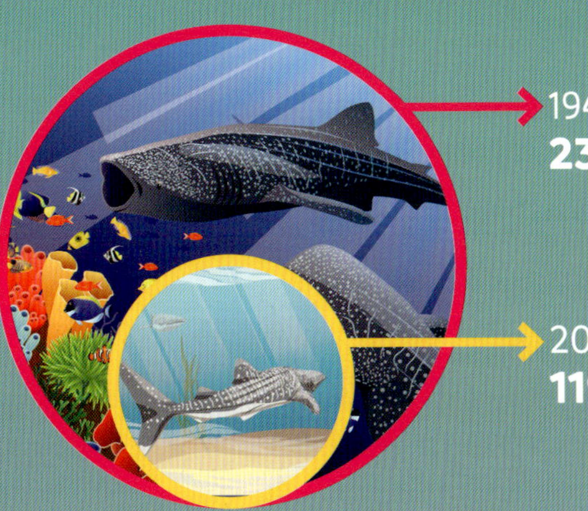

1947 Whale Shark Population
238,000–476,000

2002 Whale Shark Population
119,000–238,000

*Estimate

Whale Shark Quiz

1 Is the whale shark a whale or a shark?

2 How fast does a whale shark typically swim?

3 How long do most adult whale sharks live?

4 At what age is a female whale shark believed to have her first pups?

5 How many young can a female shark be pregnant with at once?

6 What does a whale shark eat?

7 What are some threats causing whale shark numbers to decrease?

8 How thick can the skin of an adult whale shark be?

ANSWERS **1.** A whale shark is a shark, which means it is also a fish. **2.** 3 to 5 miles (5 to 8 km) per hour **3.** About 70 years **4.** About 30 years old **5.** More than 300 **6.** Fish, eggs, and plankton **7.** Being caught by fishers, being hit by boats, and swallowing plastics **8.** 4 inches (10 cm)

Key Words

camouflage: coloring used to hide something in its surroundings

cartilage: a strong, flexible material that forms part of some animals' bodies

endangered species: a group of animals or plants at risk of no longer existing

equator: an imaginary line that circles the Earth halfway between the North and South Poles

filters: materials that remove solids from liquids and gases

flexible: able to bend without breaking

migrate: to move from one place to another

plankton: very small plants and animals that float in lakes and seas

predators: animals that live by hunting other animals for food

range: the area in which an animal lives

solitary: living alone

subtropical: relating to regions just north or just south of the tropics

tropical: relating to places near the equator

Index

Atlantic Ocean 7

diving 7

food 9, 11, 12, 15

gills 12, 15

Indian Ocean 7

migrate 9, 11

mouth 12, 15

Pacific Ocean 7, 11

population 21

pups 17, 19, 22

skin 19, 22

weight 4

Get the best of both worlds.

AV2 bridges the gap between print and digital.

The expandable resources toolbar enables quick access to content including **videos**, **audio**, **activities**, **weblinks**, **slideshows**, **quizzes**, and **key words**.

Animated videos make static images come alive.

Resource icons on each page help readers to further **explore key concepts**.

Published by Lightbox Learning Inc.
276 5th Avenue, Suite 704 #917
New York, NY 10001
Website: www.openlightbox.com

Library of Congress Control Number: 2022942601

ISBN 978-1-7911-4524-8 (hardcover)
ISBN 978-1-7911-4525-5 (softcover)
ISBN 978-1-7911-4526-2 (multi-user eBook)

Printed in Guangzhou, China
1 2 3 4 5 6 7 8 9 0 26 25 24 23 22

082022
101121

Project Coordinator: Heather Kissock
Designer: Terry Paulhus

Photo Credits
Every reasonable effort has been made to trace ownership and to obtain permission to reprint copyright material. The publisher would be pleased to have any errors or omissions brought to its attention so that they may be corrected in subsequent printings. Lightbox Learning acknowledges Getty Images, Alamy, Shutterstock, and Dreamstime as its primary image suppliers for this title.